REVELATION
TODAY

BY JOHN BRADSHAW

IT IS WRITTEN

ISBN: 978-1-937173-05-0

Contents

ONE

Light for a Dark World

I'll never forget how dark it was. My family and I were caving with friends in Kentucky. We were exploring a "wild" cave on private land, not a commercial cave with guided tours, such as you'd find at Mammoth Cave or Luray Caverns.

Those guiding us were experienced with this cave system and knew their way around it. And of course, we were caving with the benefit of caving lights and helmet lamps. But when we turned those lights off deep underground, it suddenly became *dark*—so dark you couldn't see your hand an inch in front of your face. You could almost feel the darkness. We all recognized how fortunate we were to have light. Without light, there was absolutely no way in the world we would ever be able to find our way out of the cave—it simply wouldn't be possible.

What a relief it was to know that all we had to do was turn on our helmet lights, and we would be okay. But without the benefit of the light, we were completely helpless, stuck in the most total darkness any of us had ever experienced.

Similarly, we currently live in a dark world, perhaps the darkest it has ever been since time began. Ours is an age of materialism, post-modernism, cynicism, and spiritualism. Society is darkened by crime and vice, substance abuse and child abuse, aggression, depression, oppression, and recession.

Financially, the planet seems to teeter on the brink of ruin. The vast majority of news we hear about the environment is that the world is flirting with calamity, and earthquakes and other natural disasters bring chaos on a scale never before seen in the modern world. Socially, experts tell us that we have a generation of kids that, while connected electronically, are disconnected emotionally and consume pharmaceuticals in record quantities. A doom merchant might have good reason to proclaim that there's no way out of the planet's darkness.

Except for one thing. The light.

The God of heaven has left us with a light. Jesus, the Light of the world, came to planet Earth two millennia ago to save humanity from its depravity (Mt. 1:21), and to reveal to the world the character of His heavenly Father (Jn. 14:9). And He left us His holy Word, the Bible, described by David as "a lamp unto my feet and a light unto my path" (Ps. 119:105).

In the Old Testament we find the history of the creation of the world, the calling of God's people, the lives and example of the patriarchs and the prophets, the giving of God's law, and God's justice and tender care in guiding the Israelites to the Promised Land and beyond.

The New Testament introduces us to Jesus, the promised Messiah, who was born in a manger, raised in obscurity, and persecuted by the religious establishment. Much of the New Testament tells the story of the early Christian church and of how God guided a dozen men to ultimately take the message of salvation to the world.

And then God's Word has special light for those living in the last days of earth's history. The final book of the Bible is the book of Revelation, which God says was written to show His people "things which must shortly come to pass" (Rev. 1:1). As God guided the Old Testament church through the ministry of the prophets and judges, and as He guided the New Testament church through the ministry of the apostles and prophets, God seeks to specially guide His church today through the book of Revelation.

The book of Revelation was written as "the Revelation of Jesus Christ" (Rev. 1:1). While many people are confused, almost dazed, by the book of Revelation, God intended it to be a special source of guidance and encouragement for His people waiting for the return of Jesus.

The third verse of the book of Revelation says, "Blessed is he who reads, and they that hear the words of this prophecy, and keep those things which are written therein: for the time is at hand." But such a statement doesn't square with what many people teach about the book of Revelation.

Many years ago, while I was holding a Bible prophecy seminar in a small town in central

Kentucky, a man told me that his Sunday School teacher told him the book of Revelation is "nothing more than a Stephen King novel tucked into the back of the Bible." The fact is, nothing could be farther from the truth. While it is true that parts of the book of Revelation can be challenging to understand—a beast with seven heads and ten horns, a lamb with seven heads and seven eyes, plagues and seals and thunders and trumpets—the book of Revelation contains light especially calculated by God to guide His people out of the darkness of this world and into the glorious light of His eternal presence.

In this book, you're going to discover how the Bible's book of Revelation is practical and relevant and how God speaks in the book of Revelation to help prepare us for the most momentous events in the history of the planet. It seems forgotten by the majority of Christians that the book of Revelation is the "Revelation of Jesus Christ," and one might think that a book that reveals Jesus is the very book we need to guide us in this sin-darkened world.

The world is in a mess. The enemy of souls is at the top of his game. Everywhere we look, we see evidence that Satan continues to tighten his grip on this world.

While this book isn't intended to be a commentary on the entire book of Revelation, it will examine some of the key points of Revelation and explore its major themes. And a vitally important truth of the book of Revelation is that it is given to reveal Christ. Far from it being "nothing more than a Stephen King book," it is a book whose time has come—a book with a message that is urgently needed now.

The book of Revelation has for too long been misunderstood—being the target of critics and naysayers, sensationalists and speculators. Correctly understood—among the beasts and horns and signs and symbols—Revelation shines brightly, providing light to a world shrouded with darkness. Revealing the love of God, providing gracious guidance, sounding necessary warnings about impending spiritual danger, God offers light in a darkened world, light given to lead us into the eternal embrace of a loving God.

Speaking to the heart of humanity and addressing the longings of a wayward world, God's voice continues to be heard. And His voice *will* be heard, as we take the time to carefully consider the last book of the Bible—the "Revelation of Jesus Christ."

TWO

Unexpected Value

A lady was walking one morning in New York City, when she spotted something brightly colored in a pile of trash on the sidewalk. Curious, she examined the trash and discovered that the brightly colored object was actually a painting. Thinking it didn't seem right for a piece of art to be discarded, she took the painting back to her apartment and in time inquired about the painting's origins. She eventually discovered that the artwork was a painting by Mexican artist Rufino Tamayo and had been stolen twenty years earlier. Returned to its original owners, it was later sold at auction for more than a million dollars. An extremely valuable work of art had been languishing in the trash and was headed for a landfill!

Too many people consider the book of Revelation to be of little more worth than trash on a sidewalk, and they hurry past it without taking the time to look at it and understand its true value. Valuable, it is. The "Revelation of Jesus Christ," it exists to point us to the One who is so valuable that He is described as the "Pearl of great price"—more valuable than silver or gold.

A key point about the book of Revelation is that, as important as they are, there is more to Revelation than beasts and horns. Revelation is the book of the Lamb. It really is Jesus' book, and as you read it, you'll meet Him there, and He'll bless your life.

The book of Revelation is the book of the Bible especially written for the final days of earth's history. And just five verses into the book of Revelation, we find the first portrayal of Jesus found in the 404 verses that make up the Bible's final book. After four verses of introduction, John writes, "Unto Him who loved us, and washed us from our sins in His blood." Barely into the book of Revelation—a book that some claim is a "closed" or "sealed" book—John introduces his friend Jesus as the Savior of the world.

John describes Jesus as One who has loved the world. Even that simple fact is important, as there are many people who don't realize that Jesus takes a personal, loving interest in this world. Jesus isn't detached from the reality of our daily lives or from what is going on here on earth. He loves us.

And John points out that He "washed us from our sins in His blood." Here's a key point. One of the first things the book of Revelation does—a book confused by so many and shrouded in mystery—is to introduce Jesus as the Savior of the world and explain the means by which eternal life can be received by the sinner. Jesus is the Savior of the world—He "washed us from our sins." The good news of the gospel is found in the fifth verse of the book of Revelation: Jesus is the Savior of the world.

This verse shows us how salvation comes to fallen human beings. Tragically, all over the world are people whose religion is little more than a form of slavery. In many pagan religions, people attempt to appease hard-to-please gods, and in many Christian faiths, believers aren't sure how to "get" salvation from Jesus.

Many people believe that salvation comes through trying to be good enough, or that it can be gained through penances or pilgrimages or good works or offerings. As good as some of those things might be, they are not what bring cleansing and re-creation into our lives. Jesus, the Light of a dark world, brings salvation to us through His blood. That is, by His death, He paid the penalty for our sins. We can't pay the penalty ourselves, and we can't earn salvation. As a gift, we receive it by faith from the Savior of the book of Revelation.

Though the typical Christian might not know it, the book of Revelation focuses on salvation through Jesus Christ. Revelation 3:20 sees Jesus knocking on the door of the human heart, seeking admission so that He can come into the heart and change the life. Revelation 7 has the saved being sealed with the seal of God. Revelation 14 talks about God's saints, and Revelation ends with God's people reigning with Him in a land where there is no more sin.

Did God know how much we'd need assurance down here in the close of time regarding salvation from sin, and how much we'd need His work of transformation in our lives? I think He did. In a time when there has never been so much sin, God assures this world by telling us in the book of Revelation that there is a way out of sin and guilt and shame—and that way is through Jesus.

In Revelation 1:7, we see another portrait of Jesus. "Behold He cometh with clouds, and every eye shall see Him." Just seven verses into the book of Revelation—a book ignored even by many Christians—there's a portrayal of the greatest event in all of human history since the incarnation of Christ. The Old Testament spoke to this event around 300 times, and here it is mentioned in the very opening verses of the book of Revelation.

And why is that? It's because a key theme of the book of Revelation—along with that of Jesus being the great Savior of all the world—is the hope of the return of Jesus to a hurting world. The Second Coming of Jesus is mentioned again in Revelation, 14:14:

> "And I looked, and behold a white cloud, and upon the cloud one sat like unto the Son of man, having on His head a golden crown, and in His hand a sharp sickle. And another angel came out of the temple, crying with a loud voice to Him that sat on the cloud, Thrust in thy sickle, and reap: for the time is come for thee to reap; for the harvest of the earth is ripe. And He that sat on the cloud thrust in His sickle on the

earth; and the earth was reaped" (Revelation 14:14–16).

And then in Revelation 19, we see another picture of Jesus coming back to this world—one of the most stunning passages of Scripture you'll find.

> "And I saw heaven opened, and behold a white horse; and He that sat upon Him was called Faithful and True, and in righteousness He doth judge and make war. His eyes were as a flame of fire, and on His head were many crowns; and He had a name written, that no man knew, but He Himself. And he was clothed with a vesture dipped in blood: and His name is called The Word of God... And He hath on His vesture and on His thigh a name written, King of Kings, and Lord of Lords" (Revelation 19:11-13,16).

Did God know that in the twenty-first century, with all of its difficulties and burdens and complexities and pressures, that people would need hope? Did God know that the hope of the return of Jesus would enable a person to see beyond the darkness and the difficulties of this world? Yes, He did. So He made the subject of the Second Coming of Jesus a major point of emphasis in the book of Revelation. He hasn't forgotten about this world, He hasn't forgotten about you, and He is coming back soon to end the sin and the tragedy and the heartbreak experienced in a world where sin continues to do its deadly work.

If you choose to, you can be intimidated by seals and trumpets as you read the book of Revelation, and you can do battle with thunders and plagues. And I'm not suggesting those things are not important. They're very important, which is why God had them included in the book of Revelation. But before you write off Revelation and put it in the "too tough" basket, remember what it's about. A main theme of Revelation is the Second Coming of Jesus. God tells you in Revelation that there is hope for you, because Jesus is coming soon.

Revelation majors in the ideas, themes and thoughts that matter to all of us: Jesus, the Savior; Jesus, the coming King.

The book opens with John writing that it is "the Revelation of Jesus Christ." Who is this Jesus who is revealed? Revelation calls Him the Alpha and the Omega (Revelation 1:8). *Alpha* and *Omega* are the first and last letters of the Greek alphabet—and Revelation was originally written in Greek. So John is calling Jesus the "beginning and the end"—the "A" and the "Z," you could say. Revelation calls Jesus "the bright and morning star" (Revelation 22:16) and "the Lion of the tribe of Judah" (Revelation 5:5)—the great, mighty conquering One. He is the "Lamb as it had been slain" (Revelation 5:6), the humble servant who went meekly to His death so we could live forever. He is the One "who walks in the midst of [the churches]" (Revelation 2:1).

Revelation depicts Jesus as "the Son of God" (Revelation 2:18), "the faithful and true Witness" (Revelation 3:14), and the "King of Kings and Lord of Lords" (Rev. 19:16). Amidst the symbols and signs, there's a Savior, Jesus, who wants to be known, because if people get to know Jesus for themselves, lives will be changed, and the world in which we live would be a better place.

Among the many portraits of Jesus in the book of Revelation, we find this one in chapter 14: John writes, "worship Him who made the heavens and the earth and the sea and the fountains of waters" (Rev. 14:7).

In earth's last conflict we are reminded that Jesus is this world's Creator. John 1:3 says that "all things were made by Him, and without Him was not anything made that was made," and you read virtually the same thing in Colossians 1:16. This is not to say Jesus did all of this independent of the Father and the Holy Spirit. But the Bible credits Jesus as being the active agent in creation, and when we're called to worship Him, we are called to worship Him as the Creator.

This is God's reassurance to a skeptical world— a post-modern world, an unbelieving world— that we didn't get here by accident. We're not the result of random processes. Jesus is helping us understand our true value as those formed in the image of God and created to live forever— "fearfully and wonderfully made," as the psalmist wrote in Psalm 139:14. The idea that humanity is simply the result of a freak, chance occurrence robs the race of its true identity and its real worth. And in the last book of the Bible, God emphasizes the point that Jesus is the Creator, and we are to worship Him as such.

Revelation tells us that we are the works of His hands, made for specific purposes—to know and serve God, to realize our full potential in Christ, to put off sin and all things that are destructive, and to put on Jesus and live lives of eternal worth.

Some years ago, a couple was given a painting as a housewarming gift. In 2008, wanting to have the painting appraised for insurance purposes, the woman of the house to whom it was given brought it to a screening of the PBS television program "Antiques Roadshow." She was shocked to discover that the painting, by Clyfford Still—one of the founders of the Abstract Expressionist movement—was worth at least half a million dollars! She had no idea what the painting was worth, and beamed when told of its actual value.

The value of the book of Revelation is a mystery to many people. When we discover that it directs us to Jesus and presents Him as the Hope for all humanity—its Savior, Redeemer, Creator, and coming King—the value of the book is more clearly seen. Not a book to be neglected and discarded, it was given us by God to be truly "the revelation of Jesus Christ."

THREE

The Seven Churches

I consider myself fortunate to have grown up going to church. And it wasn't just because we lived just five doors down from the church that we attended every week. Church was important to us. We never missed. As an altar boy (an assistant to the parish priest), there was a time when I attended church every *day* for two and a half years. I attended a church school, attended "extra" church events with my dad, and prayed every night before I went to sleep.

At church, I learned a lot that was good and helpful—much that instilled in me a desire to know Jesus more. Mine was a good church. It wasn't a perfect church by any means, but by most measures, it was a good church.

Down through history, Jesus has never had a perfect church. The church He was a member of while He lived on earth was responsible for His death. The leaders of the church He established on earth after He died were far from perfect—

impetuous Peter; James and John, the "sons of thunder"; doubting Thomas; and Paul, the rehabilitated persecutor of God's people.

What made the church effective, usable, and an effective instrument in the hands of God, was its submission to the leadership of God through the leading of the Holy Spirit. Filled with God's Spirit, impetuous Peter became a powerful preacher (Acts 2:14–39) and a bold witness for God (Acts 4:19, 20). John, who at one time was prepared to incinerate those who disagreed with him (Luke 9:54) went on to heal the blind, spread the gospel, and write five books of the Bible. Paul, who stood by holding the coats of the men who stoned the martyr Steven (Acts 7:58) became a miracle-working, good news-preaching, church-planting missionary who ultimately gave his life for his faith in Christ.

When the church was led by people who were in turn led by God, it did great things for God and grew dramatically. But not long after Jesus ascended to heaven, the church began to regress, compromise, and lose its fervent love for the truth of God's Word. Ultimately, the church reached its nadir during the Middle Ages, known also as the Dark Ages, because it was a time when the light of God's Word was virtually extinguished.

Thankfully, the church of God would not always languish in the darkness of apostasy and sin. Truth would rise again, and the great truths of the Bible that were obscured in a time of compromise would be made prominent in a time of commitment and zeal. And in Revelation, God reveals that Jesus stands with His church.

Revelation 1 presents Jesus standing in the "midst of the seven candlesticks," described by Jesus as being "the seven churches" (Rev. 1:13, 20). What an assurance to believers throughout history that, in spite of circumstances or appearances, Jesus stands with them! Though beset by opposition and at times wracked with apostasy, this portrayal of Jesus standing in the midst of the churches is God's pledge that He will never forsake His church, described in Zechariah 2:8 as being "the apple of His eye."

With this assurance, God addresses the seven churches of Revelation. While actual churches in real geographical locations, the seven churches are believed by many scholars to also represent the church throughout history, from the time of the earliest Christians to the final days of earth's history.

The first of the seven churches in Revelation is Ephesus, located on the west coast of what was known in Bible times as Asia Minor and what is now known as Turkey. John—who wrote Revelation—is said to have died near Ephesus and was buried there. Ephesus, an important Greek center and later, a prominent Roman city, is today the site of a great number of magnificent Roman ruins.

Paul's letter to the Ephesians was written to the church in this city. In Revelation, John writes that Jesus is pleased with the Ephesians' intolerance for false teachers and commends their commitment to the ministry of the gospel (Rev. 2:2, 3). But then Jesus adds something sobering. He says, "Nevertheless, I have somewhat against thee" (Rev. 2:4).

How would it be to hear these words from Jesus? As a child growing up in my home church, I was aware that our church wasn't heaven on earth, but I'd have been shocked to know that Jesus had something against us!

Jesus elaborates: "Nevertheless, I have somewhat against thee, because thou hast left thy first love" (Rev. 2:4).

The light that had burned so brightly when the Ephesians first embraced the message of salvation in Jesus had begun to dim. Like the husband who no longer buys flowers for his wife and begins to treat her with less respect than his marriage vows outline, the Ephesians drew back from the initial love they had for Jesus.

But Jesus spoke to the Ephesian church with hopefulness. He says, "Remember therefore from whence thou art fallen, and repent, and do the first works; or else I will come unto thee quickly, and remove thy candlestick out of his place, except thou repent"(Revelation 2:5).

"Except thou repent." That is, "Unless you make a turnaround, amend your ways, and become—with God's help—the believers you used to be."

In the letters to the seven churches, Jesus is gracious enough to tell the believers what they need to hear in order to be truly connected to Him. And He is gracious enough to commend them and affirm the good He sees in them. He commends the Ephesians for their commitment to the honesty and integrity seen in their ministry and for theological orthodoxy among the believers. Their intolerance of the Nicolaitans—

a group which promoted an antinomian, or "no law" theology—Jesus praised.

The conditions Jesus described and that John wrote about in this brief letter to the Ephesian church not only speak to the condition of the church in that city at the time the letter was written, but also to the condition of the early Christian church in the hundred years or so after the death of Jesus. And clearly, there is counsel in that letter to believers of all ages: Don't sanction false teachers or false teachings, uphold the claims of God's law, and repent and return to your first love—to that time when your love for Jesus was deep and strong.

The second church Jesus addresses in Revelation was the church located in Smyrna, slightly northwest of Ephesus. The name *Smyrna* comes from an ancient Greek word meaning "myrrh"—a sweet-smelling incense that was one of the gifts the Wise Men brought to baby Jesus shortly after His birth. The church of Smyrna, it is said, represents a period of Christian history during which the church suffered intense persecution (from A.D. 100 or so to shortly after A.D. 300). Their faithfulness to God during this time was as a sweet-smelling incense. After affirming the church at Smyrna, Jesus encourages them not to "fear any of those things which you are about to suffer," warning them that difficult times were ahead for the church. The "ten days" of tribulation they would endure corresponds with the ten years of intense persecution the church endured during the reign of the Roman Emperor Diocletian.

Jesus had words of consolation for the church

at Smyrna, saying, "Be faithful until death, and I will give you the crown of life."

This account seems to fit perfectly with the experience of the persecuted church of the early centuries A.D., and offers encouragement to a last-day church living on the precipice of what Daniel described as a "time of trouble such as never was" (Dan. 12:1).

Jesus states that He has "a few things against" the church at Pergamos—a compromising church that began to allow Bible truth to be mixed with theological error. The Pergamos church is said to "have there those who hold the doctrine of Balaam," a prophet who sought to put stumbling blocks in the way of God's people back in the book of Numbers. This church, unlike the church of Ephesus, tolerated the anti-law faction that sought to minimize the claims of God on the lives of church members.

The church at Pergamos receives a stern warning from Jesus. "Repent, or else I will come unto thee quickly and will fight against them with the sword of my mouth" (Rev. 2:16). Undoubtedly, Jesus knew that a direct appeal to the Pergamos church was necessary. Looking forward, He knew the state the church would be in if it continued to drift from doctrinal purity and submission to the will of God.

The church of Pergamos, relating to the period of church history when Christianity compromised with paganism and the corrupting influence of the state (around A.D. 300 to approximately A.D. 530), stands as a warning to Christians today. Compromise with untruth is spiritually deadly. Rejecting the authority and the protecting influence of the Word of God is to invite spiritual ruin. Pergamos demonstrated that, especially in the manner by which they paved the way for the spiritual darkness that followed the Pergamos time period.

The church in Thyatira receives a brief commendation from Jesus, before receiving a withering rebuke. "I have a few things against you, because you allow that woman Jezebel, who calls herself a prophetess, to teach and seduce my servants and eat things sacrificed to idols." To this church, Jesus issues a solemn warning:

> "[I will cast] those who commit adultery with her into great tribulation, unless they repent of their deeds. I will kill her children with death, and all the churches shall know that I am He who searches the minds and hearts. And I will give to each one of you according to your works" (Rev. 2:22, 23).

It's a good idea here to remember that Jesus infrequently speaks in such grave tones. How serious must the spiritual peril of the church of Thyatira have been for Jesus to speak so directly? The church in Thyatira represents that period of history when the Christian church descended into abject spiritual darkness. In terms of the growth of the Christian church and the spread of the gospel, and in terms of Satan's prospects to achieve complete domination over the only movement on the planet that can take the light of the gospel to the world—the church—this darkness spelled ruin for the world.

Of note here is the spiritual or symbolic nature of much of the book of Revelation. The seven churches were literal churches, but in the larger sense, they were symbolic of periods of time throughout church history. And as Jesus spoke to the church at Thyratira, He demonstrated clearly how God uses signs and symbols in this last-day book of the Bible. The reference to Jezebel is too clear to miss.

God chose an effective symbol from history— the hideously wicked woman Jezebel—and used that symbol to teach some powerful lessons. In the Bible, a woman is often used as a prophetic symbol to represent a *church* (Jer. 6:2; 2 Cor. 11:2). God uses a simple symbol to teach a profound truth: In the period of history that reached from around A.D. 500 to A.D. 1500, a corrupt church did to Christianity what Jezebel achieved in Israel. It incorporated unbiblical, pagan practices into the worship of God, diverting God's people from the truth of His Word and attaching their affections to mistruths and errors. In other words, apostasy was ushered into the Christian faith, and what resulted was seen in the history of the church of Thyatira.

The next of the churches Jesus addressed in Revelation was the church at Sardis. (Of interest is that the order of the seven churches in Revelation is a logical progression, following the obvious route a person would take if he or she started in Ephesus with the intention of visiting all seven locations.) The church at Sardis was a church about which Jesus could say very little of a positive nature. He described the church as having "a name that you are alive, but you are dead" (Rev. 3:1). There were only "a few names even in Sardis who have not defiled their garments," Jesus said (Rev. 3:4), representing a time of almost complete apostasy. And perhaps more alarmingly, Satan's complete victory over the Christian church looked assured at this point.

Between the 1500s and 1700s, it appeared that the church was about to give way completely to the corrupting influences of falsehood and unfaithfulness. Yet we remember that God had promised He would have a people ready to meet Jesus at the Second Coming (Jn. 14:3), and as John wrote in 1 John 4:4, "greater is He that is in you, than he that is in the world." Jesus stands in the midst of the churches!

The church of Philadelphia was proof that God still had a people who would be faithful in a time of spiritual crisis.

"I have set before you an open door, and no one can shut it; for you have a little strength, and have not defiled my name" (Revelation 3:8). Like the faithful few at the time of the Flood in Noah's day, mercy was offered to this church, which had kept His "command to persevere."

The message to the church in our day is clearly apparent. Even in a time of great spiritual darkness—a time soon to come to our world—Jesus urges His people to hang in there with Him and allow Him to "keep you from the hour of trial which shall come upon the whole world, to test those who dwell on the earth." While these words were no doubt encouraging to the church in Philadelphia, they'll one day be a source of encouragement to His end-time people living in a time of oppressive spiritual darkness. Though there be only a few faithful souls as in the Philadelphian church, God encourages His people to lean on Jesus and trust in Heaven's hand of blessing and love.

The final church addressed in the letters to the seven churches is the church of Laodicea. The word *Laodicea* means "a people judged," and the time period represented by the Laodicean church is the time of heaven's final judgment—the final days of earth's history starting in the mid-1800s, when the judgment-hour message was proclaimed during the great Second Advent movement that swept the United States.

The trouble with the church of Laodicea isn't that it is cold toward God, but that it is lukewarm. Jesus describes the problem, when He says, "You are neither cold nor hot. I could wish that you were cold or hot" (Rev. 3:15). Remarkably, Jesus says that being cold toward Him isn't the worst spiritual condition a person can experience. There's something worse.

> "So then, because you are lukewarm, and neither cold no hot, I will vomit you out of my mouth. Because you say, 'I am rich, have become wealthy, and have need of nothing'—and do not know that you are miserable, poor, blind and naked (Rev. 3:16, 17)."

The water supply of the ancient city was brought from the hot mineral springs of Hierapolis, several miles away. By the time the water arrived in Laodicea, it was lukewarm. This metaphor aptly describes the modern church, plagued by laxity and "lukewarmness" in its approach to God—a careless, self-deceived experience that substitutes theory for experiential godliness.

Worth noticing too is that in the case of each of the seven churches, God makes a special promise to those who are faithful to Him. God promised the faithful in Ephesus that they would "eat from the tree of life" (Rev. 2:7). The saints of Smyrna were assured they would "not be hurt by the second death" (Rev. 2:11), while the triumphant in Pergamos are told they would be given "some of the hidden manna to eat, and I will give him a white stone, and on the stone a new name written" (Rev. 2:17).

Those from Thyatira who continue to trust in God are given "power over the nations" and are given "the morning star" (Rev. 2:26, 28), while the faithful from Sardis will not only "walk with me in white", Jesus says, but are "clothed in white garments." The church at Philadelphia was promised the privilege of being made "a pillar in the temple of My God" (Rev. 3:12), while the faithful of Laodicea are invited by Jesus to "sit with me in my throne" (Rev. 3:21).

Clearly, Jesus cares deeply for His church, assuring His people down through time—and assuring us in these last days that He watches tenderly over His people and that their struggles and difficulties do not escape His gaze. And in chronicling the rise and fall of His church down through time, Jesus demonstrates that in the absence of a "perfect" church, God has honest souls who, in spite of their failings, are willing to take hold of Him by faith and allow His will to be done in their lives.

And that's the story of the book of Revelation. Erring human beings, united with the power of the perfection of Jesus Christ, are prepared by the Holy Spirit to leave this world and "enter in through the gates into the city" (Rev. 22:14). And by His grace, you and I can be in that group.

FOUR

How to Understand the Book of Revelation

I was passing through Tokyo on my way home to the United States, and with a couple of hours to spare, I decided to access the Internet and contact my family. I found an Internet hotspot in the Narita airport and opened my laptop and my web browser, only to find that everything that appeared on the screen was written in Japanese. I was sure that there'd be at least *something* written in English. I quickly realized I was a fish out of water.

At the airport, virtually everything was written in Japanese, and apart from a McDonald's—and a radio in a cafe playing "Isn't She Lovely?" by Stevie Wonder, which seemed oddly out of place—I was out of my depth. And now I had a computer screen that wouldn't speak to me in a language I could understand.

I adventurously clicked on a few links, in the hope that one of them would lead me to a place where I could navigate my way to communication, but it wasn't until I asked a kind Japanese man standing next to me if he could help that I finally could make sense of my online experience.

Thankfully, this man's English was nearly perfect. In fact, he lived in the United States.

"Would you please help me connect to the Internet, *in English?*" I asked.

"Oh, sure," he said. "No problem. All you need to do is click up here...where it says, 'English'!"

Sure enough, in the top right-hand corner of the screen was the word *English,* as plain as day. And when I clicked on that word, like magic, everything on the screen appeared in English, and moments later I was chatting online with my wife.

What I needed was a way to translate the Japanese on my screen. The Japanese itself was perfect. The problem was that I couldn't understand it. And until I learned the key to interpreting this foreign language, there was no way I could make any sense of what was on my screen.

And that's the experience many people have with the book of Revelation. What is written in the book is perfectly good. As with all Scripture, it was "given by inspiration of God" (2 Tim. 3:16), so any problem a reader might have isn't with the book of Revelation, but rather with the method of understanding employed.

Some choose to read Revelation as they might read a newspaper, and before long, they realize that this method of interpretation doesn't work too well. For much of the narrative, regular reading will work well enough, but once you read about a beast rising up out of the sea with seven heads and ten horns, you quickly realize that a literal reading of the book of Revelation will only get you so far.

So how is the book of Revelation to be read and understood? You might expect that there is no pithy answer to this question. Revelation is a big book, with twenty-two chapters made up of 404 verses. It was written almost 2,000 years ago by one of Jesus' closest companions, who at the time of writing was under arrest on the island of Patmos—a prisoner of the Roman Empire on account of his faith in God. And in coming to a book like Revelation, we need to remember that it was written under the inspiration of the Holy Spirit. In Isaiah 55:9, God said, "For as the heavens are higher than the earth, so are my ways higher than your ways, and my thoughts than your thoughts." Peter wrote in 2 Pet. 3:16 that the Apostle Paul wrote "things hard to be understood." So to imagine that deciphering the book of Revelation will be a walk in the theological park is unrealistic.

When reading the book of Revelation, it's important to realize that almost two-thirds of its verses contain quotes from, or references or allusions to, the Old Testament Scriptures. The "Bible" John had at his disposal was the Old Testament, the frame of reference for many of the people who would read Revelation. So John used the language and the imagery of the Old Testament to convey his message to his readers. By using a few words of Old Testament imagery, John could make a comprehensive point and communicate powerful spiritual truths to his readers.

Revelation relies heavily on the use of symbols and images based upon the Old Testament Scriptures. Understanding the symbols can't be done, independently of their origin. And this is what John intended. The symbols of Revelation are to be unlocked with the keys given us in the Old Testament.

When it comes to interpreting the book of Revelation, there are two main schools of interpretative thought. Futurism holds that the vast majority of the prophecies in the book of Revelation are yet to be fulfilled (that they will be fulfilled in the "future"). Preterism posits that the major prophecies of Revelation have been fulfilled already (that they have been fulfilled *previously*).

The futurist school of prophetic interpretation holds that the antichrist is an as-yet-unknown figure whose identity will be revealed in the future. Which means that the prophecies regarding the two beasts of Revelation 13—the one after which the entire world wonders, and the beast who causes the world to follow the first beast—are, at best, matters open to conjecture and opinion.

Preterists contend that the antichrist nation of Revelation 13 has already appeared on and disappeared from the world stage, and was—in the opinion of many preterists—the Roman Emperor Nero. I recall teaching prophecy in a seminar in California some years ago when some students from a local seminary challenged me on my interpretation of the book of Daniel.

"Pastor John," they protested, "you can't place

Daniel 7 and the rise of the little horn in the last days! All of that was fulfilled centuries ago!"

You can see the cleverness of Satan's tactics. Looking through the lens of either of these two schools of prophetic interpretation, the book of Revelation is largely devoid of practical meaning for people living today. Either everything in the book has happened and is now just an historical footnote, or little of the book of Revelation has yet been fulfilled, and it can't be understood in the light of historical precedent. Either it is old hat—or we have a guessing game. Either way, it can have little bearing on life in today's world.

Thankfully, there's a third method of interpreting the prophecies of the book of Revelation, and that's what is known as the "historicist" view of prophetic interpretation. Historicism connects prophecy with actual historical events and figures, suggesting that end-time prophecies can be related to events that have already taken place. Therefore, in looking forward to prophecies yet to be fulfilled, Bible students can find historical precedents to guide our understanding of future events.

For example, the seven churches mentioned in Revelation 2 and 3 are all real churches that existed in a historical context. The seven trumpets and the seven seals—which appear to deal with events of significance as relates to God's church down through the ages—can be best understood by studying them in connection with historical events. Such an approach would consider the seals and trumpets to have been largely, though not entirely, fulfilled.

Revelation 12 spans all of human history, from the time of the fall of Satan and his eviction from heaven (Rev. 12:7–9) to the time of his last-day attack on God's people (Rev. 12:17).

When we look at Revelation 13, which deals with the end-time beast, the manner in which we choose to interpret this prophecy becomes crucial to a correct understanding of God's Word. The Bible says that the beast will be "worshipped" (verse 4), will persecute God's people (verse 7), and will have a "mark" of authority that brings spiritual ruin to those who receive it (verse 16).

If all of this is a matter of history, as suggested by the preterist view, then the prophecy is merely of academic interest. If the chapter pertains to events to occur in the distant future, the prophecies it contains have little to say to Bible students of today, and any attempt to understand the identity of the primary figures in the chapter is virtually futile.

However, when the chapter is considered from an *historical* perspective, it can be clearly understood.

A direct connection is seen between the heads and horns of verse 1 and the beasts (nations) in Daniel 7—and the horns in Dan. 7:7.

Many historians teach that the beasts in Daniel 7 represent Babylon (the lion with eagle's wings), Medo-Persia (the bear), Greece (the leopard) and Rome (the "dreadful" beast which has "ten horns"). So one could safely assume that the beast with ten horns in Revelation 13 is connected somehow to the beast in Daniel 7 which has ten horns—Rome.

And as Revelation 13 is studied, it is discovered that many of the events portrayed in the chapter—the beast's mortal wound (verse 3), the great power of the beast (verse 4), the committing of blasphemy (verse 5), 42 months of rule (verse 5) and the persecution of God's people (verse 7)—are linked to actual historical events connected to the Roman Empire and the Roman church. When those events are understood in their historical context, questions about as-yet-unfulfilled aspects of Revelation 13 become easier to answer.

Pushing the prophecies of the Bible back into the past or forward into the future makes Revelation virtually impossible to understand. An historicist approach to understanding Revelation's prophecies helps make sense of the Bible's last book.

So where did preterism and futurism come from? Knowing that will help us understand how we ought to approach the book of Revelation.

After the Protestant Reformation began, the Roman Catholic Church found itself the target of some pointed teaching by people such as Martin Luther, who began to expose what they considered to be the errors of the Roman church. Among other ideas, the Reformers taught that the Roman Catholic papacy was the antichrist of Bible prophecy.

The Vatican reacted to this attack on its legitimacy and authority by conducting what became known as the "Counter-Reformation." The Council of Trent—a commission of high-ranking Catholic leaders tasked with defending and redefining Catholicism—turned to a Spanish Jesuit named Francisco Ribera. Ribera was charged with defining the prophecies of the Bible so they could be interpreted in such a way as to exonerate Catholicism of the charges made against it by Luther and others.

Ribera's commentary on the book of Revelation placed the fulfillment of much of the book of Revelation in the distant future, shortly prior to the Second Coming of Jesus. Based on this theory, Luther's charge that the papacy was the antichrist of the Bible couldn't possibly be correct, as the antichrist wasn't going to appear on the world scene for many centuries.

While it took some time for Ribera's ideas to take hold, they now represent the most popularly held views in Protestantism. A Jesuit work of futurism—produced with the intention of removing Rome from consideration as the antichrist—forms the modern-day basis for Protestant understanding of the subject of the antichrist.

Another Spanish Jesuit, Luis de Alcazar, formulated the theory of preterism. Like Ribera, Alcazar formulated his ideas during the Counter-Reformation with the purpose of providing a system of prophetic interpretation that did not implicate the Roman papacy in discussions about the end-time antichrist.

Alcazar's idea was that the apocalyptic prophecies of the book of Revelation were fulfilled in the first century. Like Ribera's interpretation of Revelation, Alcazar's theories removed Rome from any discussion about the identity of the antichrist. For the most part, modern-day Protestants who subscribe to Alcazar's view on the book of Revelation don't realize that their belief is based upon an attempt—like that of Ribera—to discredit the work of the Protestant reformers.

The historicist approach to interpreting prophecy—including the book of Revelation—recognizes that some prophecy has been fulfilled, some is in the process of being fulfilled, and some will be fulfilled in the future. Such an approach to understanding Bible prophecy allows the Bible student to base his or her understanding of the future on the past fulfillment of prophecy anchored in history. While historicism doesn't remove the need for careful study of God's Word, it does eliminate the need for speculation and guesswork.

Not every comet that arcs through the sky can be Halley's Comet. But even an amateur astronomer, basing his or her conclusions on solid scientific observation, can avoid coming to faulty conclusions that have no basis in fact. If we want to correctly understand the book of Revelation, it is important to approach it from the right point of view. Historicism provides a framework for reliably understanding end-time prophecy that other schools of interpretation cannot offer, enabling us to avoid speculation and misinformation that will lead us far from the truth God has given us.

Halley's Comet last appeared in 1986. Like many others, I was eager to see this once-in-a-lifetime phenomenon and ventured out one night determined to witness something truly historic.

How thrilled I was to find a little blurry speck

in the distant sky dragging a tail behind it as it careened through space. But after a while I noticed there were other objects that looked remarkably like Halley's Comet. In fact, they looked exactly the same as what I had been looking at. Then I realized that wherever I looked in the sky, I was seeing small blurry specks with tails trailing behind.

It became evident that I hadn't been looking at Halley's Comet, after all. I never did see it—at least, not knowingly. But I learned that if you don't start with the correct information, you can end up seeing things you're not looking at.

And how true that is when it comes to studying the Bible. Many people arrive at wrong theological conclusions because they begin with a flawed premise, causing the Bible to say things it isn't actually saying.

Learning to look at Revelation in its proper context will help the Bible student to make reliable conclusions about God's Word. Just as my Japanese-language computer screen suddenly appeared in a language I could understand, the book of Revelation will become understandable, when we apply the right principles of interpretation.

FIVE

Beyond the Music

As a teenager being drawn into the world of popular music, I became fascinated with singer Don McLean's *magnum opus,* "American Pie". The song had been released when I was a child, and one day I became intrigued with its lyrics. Words such as, "The players tried to take the field, the marching band refused to yield; do you recall what was revealed the day the music died?" left me wondering what the song was all about. I found out later that the popular belief is that McLean wrote the song at least in part about the death of musician Buddy Holly— "the day the music died."

Later, I became intrigued with the sometimes-obscure lyrics of songs by Paul Simon, which I often played on the radio during my days as a broadcaster. "He is surrounded by the sound, the sound, cattle in the marketplace, scatterlings and orphanages. He looks around, around, he sees angels in the architecture, spinning in infinity; he says, Amen and Hallelujah!" (From "You Can Call Me Al".) Words such as that have to mean *something*, don't they?

What I found out later was that in many cases, the words of songs don't really mean anything at all. In the song "Me and Julio Down by the Schoolyard," Simon sang, "It's against the law, it was against the law; what the mama saw, it was against the law." When asked in an interview with *Rolling Stone* magazine in 1972 what it was that was against the law, Paul Simon said, "I have no idea... I never bothered to figure out what it was. Didn't make any difference to me."

David Byrne, once a part of the band Talking Heads, said in an interview that he considered the meaning of the words in a song to be much less important than many people think. "People ignore them half the time," he said. "In a certain way, it's the sound of the words, the inflection and the way the song is sung...that has as much of the meaning as the actual, literal words."

Of course, there are times a song's words are very meaningful, but in many cases they don't really mean a thing. A case in point: Paul Simon got the title of his hit song "Mother and Child Reunion" from a menu in a Chinese restaurant. "Mother and Child Reunion" was the name of a chicken-and-eggs dish where Simon was eating one day. He liked the phrase so much he decided to include it in a song (which was about the death of a dog), and the song—with its meaningless title phrase—almost made it to the top of the pop charts.

When it comes to the book of Revelation, one

of the first things a reader often asks is, "Do these strange things I'm reading actually *mean* anything?" A beast with seven heads and ten horns (Rev. 13:1)? Another beast with "two horns like a lamb" that "spoke like a dragon" (Rev. 13:11)? What's the meaning of words such as these?

Many have dismissed the Bible's last book as virtually meaningless (such as our friend who made the apostle John of the same ilk as novelist Stephen King). Nineteenth-century agnostic Robert Ingersoll dubbed Revelation "the insanest of all books." Many modern-day Bible teachers claim the book of Revelation has no significance for modern Christians.

But we find in Revelation chapter 13 that God opens to the understanding of end-time believers details regarding the final great spiritual battles this world will pass through. The reason for doing so is clear. In earth's final days, the planet will be subjected to spiritual confusion the likes of which has never been seen, jeopardizing the eternal future of every inhabitant. In other words, we're heading for a spiritual crisis of the first order, and in the book of Revelation God provides us with the information we need to get out of this world and into the world to come.

Revelation 13 starts with John seeing a "beast rise up out of the sea." I once met a man who lived on the coast of the state of Washington who told me that each morning he looked out over the ocean and wondered if "today would be the day the beast would come up out of the sea." Whoever this beast is, it is obviously enormously significant. Revelation 13:3, 4, and 8 says that the whole world will follow and worship this beast. Of tremendous global significance, this beast will possess more power than any ruler who has ever lived. No figure in history has ever had the worship of the entire world. Whatever or whoever this beast power is, it has to be big.

It would seem strange that God would warn the world about the biggest deception to come to the earth in thousands of years and not tell us how we can know the identity of the key players in this drama. So, who is the beast?

Actually, a better first question would be: *What* is the beast? And finding the right answer to this question is more simple than many people might think.

Keep in mind that in writing Revelation, John borrowed a lot of symbolism and imagery from the Old Testament. A significant amount of what he wrote is clearly based on the book of Daniel —a book that deals with subject matter similar to that in Revelation and that is written in a similar style. In Daniel, chapter 7, Daniel dreams of "four great beasts" that "came up from the sea" (Dan. 7:3), and later in the chapter, he explains what those beasts are. "Those great beasts, which are four, are four kings which arise out of the earth" (Dan. 7:17). In verse 23, Daniel said that the "fourth beast shall be a fourth kingdom." Daniel was very clear that a "beast" represents a "kingdom" or a nation, and when John borrowed the prophetic symbol from Daniel, he intended the same meaning.

Some years ago, I saw an internationally known television Bible commentator say with clarity and conviction that "every time the book of Revelation uses that word *beast,* it is referring to a man." But in Revelation 13, when John sees a beast coming up out of the sea, he is referring to the rise of a powerful nation. And by depicting the nation as rising out of the "sea," John is stating that the nation rose into prominence in a heavily populated part of the world. The sea represents multitudes of people (Rev. 17:15).

So in warning the world about a coming beast, John is saying that there would come a time when a nation would rise to prominence and become so powerful that it would eventually lead the world—which, surely, is not so hard to believe.

And I want you to notice what we've done in our attempt to understand the identity of Revelation 13's first beast. We've gone to the Bible and allowed the Bible to interpret itself. Rarely is there any reason to guess when it comes to interpreting Bible prophecy. Comparing one text of Scripture with another is always the best way to come to correct conclusions in studying the book of Revelation, or the whole Bible, for that matter.

The nation is depicted as having seven heads and ten horns, clearly identifying it as being of the same character as the dragon—Satan—presented in Revelation 12:3. It comprises characteristics of the pagan kingdoms Daniel viewed in Daniel 7: It is like a leopard (Greece), has the mouth of a lion (Babylon), and the feet of a bear (Medo-Persia). And the dragon—Satan—gave this nation its power, throne and great authority. The nation would recover from a deadly wound and would be followed by the entire world.

The identity of this "beast" has been the subject of much study and perhaps even more speculation. I've had people tell me this beast is former U.S. President Ronald Reagan. Why? Because each of his three names (Ronald Wilson Reagan) has six letters, standing for 6-6-6, the number of the beast. It isn't hard to see that reasoning of that nature isn't going to help a person understand the truth of God's Word. As I sit typing this, I'm less than two miles away from where former President Reagan is buried. I've been to his grave at the Ronald Reagan Presidential Library in Simi Valley, California. Let me assure you: Ronald Reagan isn't—and wasn't—the beast of Revelation.

There seems to be no end to the creative attempts to understand the identity of the beast. I've heard people say the beast is Prince Charles, heir to the British throne. The name of King Juan Carlos of Spain has also been suggested (such a ridiculous claim, that I've barely bothered to find out why it has been suggested). Former U.S. Secretary of State Henry Kissinger was said to be the beast some years ago, as was former Soviet Premier Mikhail Gorbachev—(remember the mark on his forehead? Some thought it was the mark of the beast)—and even former President Bill Clinton. Years ago it was suggested that a supercomputer at the headquarters of the United Nations in Brussels, Belgium, was nicknamed "the beast" and was therefore the beast of prophecy. Even American multinational corporation Procter & Gamble was incorrectly tagged as the antichrist of prophecy, after some people believed there was something sinister about its former corporate logo.

One simple thing prevents us from even needing to entertain these ideas. A beast represents a nation—not an individual, not a computer, and not a corporation. If we make the Bible its own interpreter, we can't possibly go in these faulty directions.

Revelation 13:5 says the beast will "continue for forty-two months"–the same period of time mentioned in Revelation 11:2 and expressed again in the next verse as 1,260 days. Rather than concluding that this nation will rule for 1,260 days, we must remember another key to interpreting Bible prophecy—that a day is used to represent a year. You'll see that in Numbers 14:34 and Ezekiel 4:6, and the principle is made obvious as it reveals the accuracy of various prophecies. So the 1,260 days the beast reigns is a period of 1,260 years—much longer than any human being has ever lived on the earth.

And a key to comprehending the identity of the beast of Revelation 13 is to recognize the key issue of the chapter. Revelation 13 shows us that the agenda of the beast is to receive *worship*. Verse 4 says, "So they worshiped the dragon who gave authority to the beast; and they worshiped the beast, saying, 'Who is like the beast? Who is able to make war with him?'" And verse 8 says, "All who dwell on the earth will worship him, whose names have not been written in the Book of Life of the Lamb slain from the foundation of the world."

If you give this the thought it deserves, the "big

picture" suddenly becomes a whole lot clearer. In fact, one reason so many people don't understand the book of Revelation as they might is because they don't see Bible prophecy's big picture. Let's think about it for a moment.

Long ago, Lucifer rebelled in heaven. As remarkable as it seems, he became discontent with his own position and with the way God was running the universe. Ultimately, Lucifer craved worship. The thought of his heart was, "I will exalt my throne above the stars of God; I will also sit on the mount of the congregation on the farthest sides of the north; I will ascend above the heights of the clouds, I will be like the Most High" (Isa. 14:13, 14). After being evicted from heaven, Lucifer—now Satan—came to the earth determined to receive here the worship he wasn't successful at receiving in heaven.

He quickly succeeded in turning the hearts of Adam and Eve away from God, and then he began developing a kingdom on earth that would stand in rebellion to the kingdom of heaven—a kingdom whose subjects would be loyal to Satan and opposed to the government of God. Satan's goal is to bring planet earth to the place where its inhabitants worship Satan and reject God's sovereignty. He is seeking worship, with the mark of the beast being the sign that people have rejected God's authority and have instead accepted Satan's authority in their lives.

So in Revelation 13, the beast is not a rogue Middle Eastern dictator or a disaffected Jewish leader, as some commentators claim. The beast is, instead, a nation that arises in a populated part of the world, rules for 1,260 years, is religious in nature, blasphemes God (Rev. 13:6), persecutes God's people (Rev. 13:7), and receives worship (Rev. 13:4, 8).

That Christianity is today in such confusion on this topic is curious. At one time, Protestant Christianity was virtually unanimous in its opinion on the identity of the first beast of the book of Revelation.

The Protestant Reformation came about as a reaction to what were perceived to be the errors and abuses of the medieval church. John Wycliffe, in the early 1400s, and Jan Hus (John Huss) strongly opposed the rampant corruption that existed in the church at that time. Martin Luther was appalled at the corruption he witnessed within the church during a trip to Italy early in the sixteenth century, and after he nailed his ninety-five theses—points on which he felt the church was in error—to the door of the castle church in Wittenberg, Germany, in late October of 1517, the Reformation began in earnest.

Although it was not his original intention, Martin Luther found himself increasingly at odds with the church. In time, Luther, along with other Reformers such as Switzerland's Ulrich Zwingli and the Frenchman John Calvin, identified the papacy—the office of the pope of the Roman Catholic Church—as being the first beast of Revelation 13. John Knox, the father of the Presbyterian Church, and John Wesley, who founded the Methodist movement, also agreed that John was discussing the papacy when writing about the first beast of Revelation 13.

Modern Protestants, curiously, have generally forgotten the teachings of their spiritual ancestors on the subject of Revelation's beast. Perhaps a question to ask is: Does the opinion of the Reformers on this subject stand up to academic and theological scrutiny?

The answer is: Yes, it does. The Vatican City—a sovereign nation—arose in populated Italy. It dominated the global political and ecclesiastical landscape for 1,260 years, before a deadly wound (the capture of Pope Pius VI in 1798) brought it temporarily to its knees. Obviously, it is a religious power, which viciously persecuted dissenters during the height of its power and will receive worship when the mark of the beast is enforced.

This does not mean that individual Roman Catholics are the "beast" of Revelation 13. John the Revelator identifies a system that has not only departed from the truths of the gospel but also endangers people spiritually, by promulgating teachings that lead people away from Christ rather than pointing people to Him.

In spite of promoting many solid spiritual values and emphasizing trust in Jesus Christ, the papacy continues to espouse teachings that unequivocally deny some of the basic tenets of Christianity. Christianity teaches that there is "one mediator between God and men, the man Christ Jesus" (1 Tim. 2:5). But Rome teaches that forgiveness for sins comes as a result of a sinner receiving absolution for his or her sins from a priest, acting "in the person of Christ." Forgiveness of sin is one of the fundamental principles in a relationship with Jesus Christ and is tightly linked to the doctrine of justification (pardon) by faith. The Bible teaches that salvation from sin comes freely (Eph. 2:8) through the forgiveness that flows from confession of sin through Jesus Christ (1 Jn. 1:9). The Catholic teaching of confession to a priest and forgiveness based upon penances performed is an unbiblical monstrosity.

Yet like several other bedrock teachings of Roman Catholicism, confession to a priest and the performing of penances has absolutely no basis in the Bible and does, in fact, remove in a great way the work of salvation from Jesus, transferring it into the hands of an earthly priest.

Many other false teachings diminish the role of Jesus and belittle the Bible teaching of salvation by faith alone. The very existence of an earthly priesthood is a denial of the biblical teaching that believers have not an earthly but a *heavenly* priest. Hebrews 8:1, 2 says, "We have such a high priest, who is seated at the right hand of the throne of the majesty in the heavens, a minister of the sanctuary, and of the true tabernacle which the Lord erected, and not man." The believer's priest is Jesus, enthroned in the heavenly sanctuary and not in an earthly church.

Consider also the teaching of praying to saints. Remember 1 Tim. 2:5: "One mediator between God and men, the man Christ Jesus." Millions of people are instructed to pray to "saints" for any number of reasons, while the Bible encourages people to pray to nobody other than the God of heaven.

The infallibility of the pope, the assumption

of Mary into heaven, praying to Mary, the veneration of relics, and transubstantiation (the idea that the bread and juice used in the communion service are the actual body and blood of Jesus) are likewise teachings that find no basis in Scripture.

Which brings us to the reason the book of Revelation identifies the first beast of chapter 13 as the papacy. It isn't that the papacy is comprised of bad people, and it isn't that Catholics are bad or insincere. What the Bible is telling us is that there will rise a power that will diminish the role of Jesus in the plan of salvation and will urge people to look away from Jesus—and to priests or saints—in receiving salvation and to rely on their own works as being meritorious in the salvation transaction. Such teachings minimize the role of Jesus Christ in salvation.

John the Baptist said of Jesus, "He must increase, but I must decrease" (Jn. 3:30), but the Vatican causes Jesus to decrease and the papacy to increase. Additionally, the teaching of divine grace coming to an individual via the sacraments—taught to be necessary for salvation—also reduces the role of Jesus in salvation. Instead of faith in Christ being the only means of salvation, Rome has included sacraments and human works in the salvation process.

Such teachings cheapen the full salvation available to believers through the simple act of faith in Jesus Christ. This is why the Bible goes to such lengths to speak of the first beast of Revelation 13 and why John and Daniel give such exhaustive information for the purposes of identifying the beast. When we understand the nature of the beast, we can understand better the enormous importance of a vital relationship with Jesus Christ that is not compromised by a reliance on human efforts or the role of mediation other that of Christ's.

Revelation 13 emphasizes Revelation's unique role as a revelation of Jesus Christ for earth's final days. Everything about Revelation 13 urges us to trust fully and only in Jesus Christ for salvation. Other entities, no matter how righteous they may seem, cannot be relied upon in any way for assistance with salvation. Only Jesus saves—not priests, not prophets, not teachers, not pastors, not churches, not governments—only Jesus. Unreserved faith in Christ, faith in His sacrifice for sinners, and trust in His power to save will alone connect us with the power of God to transform and redeem.

I was intrigued when, in 1999, the famous Cape Hatteras lighthouse was moved over half a mile inland. Since it was completed in 1870, the ocean has crept closer to the lighthouse due to shoreline erosion, so in order to preserve the iconic, 200-foot-tall lighthouse, it was removed from its base and slowly moved on railroad tracks to its new location. Simply demolishing or mothballing the lighthouse wasn't an option—it is located on Hatteras Island near what was once known as the "graveyard of the Atlantic," and in spite of modern technologies such as GPS, the lighthouse is still considered an important navigational aid. It warns marine traffic of danger and encourages ocean vessels to stay in safe water.

Revelation 13 acts as a lighthouse, urging God's people to stay away from the rocks of deception and error and to stay in the safe waters of faith and trust in Christ. As we do, we can be confident that, through Jesus, we'll safely navigate the troubled seas of this world and arrive safely on the shore of God's great salvation.

SIX

The Bible's Best-Kept Secret

When my children were very young, my wife, Melissa, and I had the opportunity to take them to my home country of New Zealand. I planned to share a couple of special surprises with them—things that had been fixtures of my upbringing that they hadn't ever been able to experience.

As we drove west of my hometown through sheep and cattle country, the children wondered where Daddy was taking them. All they knew was that it was going to be good, fun and wet. We had taken towels, so they had wondered if we were going swimming, but I had told them we weren't going to the beach. Where could we be going?

About twenty minutes after we left town, a large building came into view directly ahead.

"What's that, Dad?" they asked. The Waingaro Hotel was the only building we had seen, other than houses and farm buildings, since leaving town. The mystery intensified—they knew we weren't going to a hotel!

"Just a moment," I said. "You'll see." Immediately before the hotel, we turned into a driveway and stopped at a small office, which doubled as a store. And it was from there the children could see where Mum and Dad had taken them.

"Swimming pools!" they called out. "Dad," one of them exclaimed, *"hot* pools!" Sitting on the Pacific Ring of Fire, New Zealand is known for its thermal activity, and growing up, we often went to the Waingaro Hot Springs. Three pools: one large and warm, one smaller and much warmer, and one for children that is a bit cooler. The hot springs also boast a couple of magnificent water slides: one long and winding and the other a high-speed thrill ride straight down the side of the hill. You can imagine my children's excitement when they saw the slides!

The complex is surrounded by bush, and during my childhood, peacocks roamed the area, giving the place a relaxed, serene, away-from-it-all feel. It's fantastic. I felt like one of the luckiest kids in the world to have a place like this virtually in my backyard.

As I expected, my children—then seven and five—had a great time, but one thing they couldn't understand was why there weren't more people there.

"Dad, a place like this should be packed!" Jacob said to me. "This is something everyone should know about!"

I thought about what he said: "Something everyone should know about." And looking at it from his point of view, I completely agreed. Fun, beautiful, inexpensive, healthy—the hot springs had it all. He was right—this was something everyone should know about.

And then I put that in a spiritual context. There's a passage in the book of Revelation that everyone should know about. In fact, the Bible says that one day, everyone will know about it.

The passage contains what the Bible calls the "everlasting gospel." If you've never heard of it, you might want to ask yourself why. Read this and consider how important these words have to be.

> "And I saw another angel fly in the midst of heaven, having the everlasting gospel to preach to them that dwell on the earth, and to every nation, kindred, tongue, and people" (Rev. 14:6).

An angel—a messenger—is depicted as flying in the midst of heaven where nobody can possibly miss him, with a message that is to go to every inhabitant on earth. And the message is called the "everlasting gospel."

It seems strange to me that while virtually every Christian church on the planet claims to be preaching the gospel, precious few pay any attention at all to what the Revelation of Jesus describes as the *"everlasting* gospel." If the gospel is important at all, the "everlasting gospel"—presented in the context of earth's final crisis—must be *colossally* important. This everlasting gospel, referred to as the "eternal" gospel in some translations of the Bible, contains the final message of warning and mercy to the world.

This close to the return of Jesus, you'd have to think that the proclamation of the everlasting gospel would be the highest priority any church could have. This message, given by Jesus Himself, especially for His people living at the end of time, has to be the Bible's best-kept secret.

Why is that? Why would Christians neglect to proclaim a contemporary message that is stunningly relevant to the times in which we live? Perhaps it is because Satan doesn't want the message proclaimed. And perhaps there's something about the message that even many Christians find especially challenging.

Revelation 14 opens with a picture of the 144,000 in the presence of Jesus—the saved with the Savior. Based on what we read in Revelation 7 and 14, the 144,000 are the group of people who come through earth's final conflict triumphant and faithful to Jesus. They are sealed with the seal of God, rather than being marked with the mark of the beast. As such, they are ready to meet Jesus when He returns. They have survived the great trying time about to come upon the earth and are prepared to spend eternity with Christ. Put simply, the 144,000 is that group of people who are alive on the earth and saved, ready to meet Jesus at the Second Coming.

What follows the opening passage of Revelation 14 is a group of seven verses given to the end-time church to prepare people to be saved and not lost—to be sealed and not marked. The everlasting gospel, the message of the three angels, is the message that produces God's end-time, sealed saints.

Revelation 14:6, 7 makes clear how important the "everlasting gospel" is. The angel who brings it is "in the midst of heaven." The message is to be proclaimed to every inhabitant of planet Earth, and the angel speaks with a "loud voice." The original Greek in which this passage was written actually says that the angel spoke with a *megas phone*—a "megaphone"—which we know is something that amplifies a message.

So this message, proclaimed with unmistakable clarity, God sends at the end of time for the purpose of preparing a group of people to be saved and not lost, informed and not deceived, sealed and not marked.

What are the specifics of the message? To begin with, the angel urges people to "Fear God and give glory to Him" (Rev. 14:7), to live lives of total surrender to God, and to honor Him in every aspect of their lives. The reason for this exhortation is made clear in the same verse. "For the hour of His judgment is come."

Paul told the Corinthian church that "we must all appear before the judgment seat of Christ" (2 Cor. 5:10), and he told the philosophers in Athens that God "has appointed a day on which He will judge the world" (Acts 17:31). The concept of a judgment day is entirely biblical. The message of the first of the three angels of Revelation 14 announces the opening of the judgment.

If we could know when the judgment was going to begin, we could know with even greater certainty the era for which the everlasting gospel message was intended. Again, we can be sure

God has not left us in the dark, when it comes to understanding a concept so obviously vital.

Keep in mind that John borrowed many of the concepts and symbols we read in the book of Revelation from the Old Testament Scriptures. In the Old Testament, judgment day occurred every year on the Day of Atonement, a Jewish feast described by one scholar as "a crisis of confession and repentance" (see Leviticus 16). Indeed, the word *judgment* comes from the Greek word *krisis,* which means "the act of judging." The Day of Atonement was a time when sins were confessed, sacrifices were offered, and the truly repentant had the blessed assurance of unity with God and the forgiveness of their sins.

When Jesus returns to earth, He will have a group of people–the 144,000, as well as those raised from the dead–ready to meet Him. Isaiah 25:9 says: "Behold, this *is* our God; we have waited for Him, and He will save us. This *is* the Lord. We have waited for Him; we will be glad and rejoice in His salvation." Paul wrote to the Thessalonians that when Jesus returns, "we who are alive and remain shall be caught up together with them in the clouds to meet the Lord in the air. And thus we shall always be with the Lord." The last-day judgment is going to determine who is prepared to meet Jesus when He returns and who of the sleeping saints will be raised at the Second Coming.

In the early to mid-1800s, a Baptist preacher named William Miller studied the prophecies of Daniel and predicted that Jesus would return in the year 1843. Miller had discovered that Daniel

8:14 said, "Unto two thousand and three hundred days, then shall the sanctuary be cleansed," which Miller took to refer to the Second Coming of Jesus. When Jesus didn't return that year, some of Miller's associates discovered an error in the way Miller calculated a time prophecy in the book of Daniel and found that Miller's original prediction should have placed the year of Jesus' return in 1844, rather than 1843.

A great revival swept the American northeast, and while many of the Baptist preacher's opponents doubted his interpretation of the Bible, nobody could doubt his math. Taking Daniel's 2,300-day prophecy, Miller rightly reckoned that because a prophetic day represented a literal year (see Numbers 14:34 and Ezekiel 4:6), Daniel 8:14 was talking about a time period of 2,300 years.

William Miller found the starting point for these 2,300 years. Daniel 9:25 gave the starting point of this great prophecy as "the going forth of the command to restore and build Jerusalem" a decree recorded in Ezra chapter 7, and dated in history as having been issued in the year 457 B.C. For Miller, it was now only a question of mathematics to determine when the Messiah would come: 2,300 years after the decree of 457 B.C., which worked out as the year 1844.

But as we know, the godly Baptist preacher's critics were right, and Jesus didn't return in 1844. But surely *something* significant had to have happened. The Bible said the sanctuary was to be cleansed. Did this not mean that Jesus would return? The mathematics of the prophecy pointed unmistakably to the year 1844. Perhaps Miller was right about the timing of the event, but wrong about the event itself.

But as some of William Miller's followers later discovered, rather than the cleansing of the sanctuary being the return of Jesus, the Word of God teaches that the cleansing of the sanctuary means only one thing: judgment day.

So while Miller's math was correct, his interpretation was not. Jesus was never going to return to the earth in 1844—but in 1844, in the courts of heaven, judgment began. The final work of determining who would be saved eternally and who would be lost eternally had to begin *sometime.* The Bible says that when Jesus returns at the Second Coming, He brings His reward with Him (Rev. 22:11), so therefore He has to determine what each person's reward will be before He returns, much as you'd determine what each family member's Christmas gift will be sometime before Christmas.

So one of the vitally important reasons for the proclamation of the everlasting gospel is that it would announce to humanity that we are living in the time of heaven's final judgment. Understanding this leads us to consider several profoundly important truths. First, Jesus is coming back soon. When the judgment is over, Jesus returns to gather the saints (Rev. 22:11) and receive them to Himself (Jn. 14:3).

Second, it must be time to stop "playing church." If Jesus is soon to return, and if He is now engaged in the work of final judgment before He returns to the earth, there can surely be no more important consideration for God's people than being ready for that great event. For thousands of years, Satan has been perfecting schemes to distract people from the important work of preparing a character that will see us out of this world and into the world to come.

When I was a child, we talked about how wonderful it would be to be able to watch your favorite movies whenever you wanted—at home! Instead of watching sports on television only on Saturday afternoons, we dreamed of being able to watch sports seven days a week. Now there are hundreds of TV channels, broadcast on satellite, cable, the Internet, and even the "old fashioned" way of broadcasting to an antenna or "rabbit ears." Add to all this Internet "surfing," smart phones and social media sites such as Facebook, and this is a distracted society. Not only can we call each other from our cell phones, but we can tweet, instant message and text virtually anywhere, anytime.

We could do none of this just a generation ago. And while these aren't bad things, they mean we're distracted. We have more entertainment choices than ever, a challenged economy demands we work harder and often longer hours, and there are more ways to spend money than there have ever been before. And when people get busy and distracted, their spiritual lives start to suffer. Now is no time to be distracted.

So God reminds us: "Fear God and give glory to Him, for the hour of His judgment has come." "Get serious," He says. If ever there was a time for people to live as though they really believed God's Word, now is certainly that time.

Third, the judgment hour message urges us to embrace Jesus fully and completely and to live a life of total commitment to Him. The Bible says that "the wages of sin is death" (Rom. 6:23), and every last person on earth has sinned (Rom. 3:23). The reality is that there's no way a person can have hope in the judgment without Jesus. 1 John 2:1 tells us that "we have an advocate with the Father, Jesus Christ the righteous," while 1 Timothy 2:5 reminds us that Jesus is the "mediator between God and men."

The Bible promises that Jesus will "save to the uttermost those who come to God through Him, since He always lives to make intercession for them" (Heb. 7:25). The word *gospel* means "good news," and news never got any better than this! Every person on earth can come to Jesus and be cleansed and saved, and in the judgment, having Jesus Christ as your personal Savior is your guarantee that the gift of eternal life is yours.

The judgment hour message is part of the "everlasting gospel"—extremely good news for anyone who would choose to trust in Jesus. He is soon to return to the earth, and all who have chosen to "fear God and give glory to Him" can face the judgment knowing they are cleansed and pardoned, "not by works of righteousness which we have done, but according to His mercy" (Titus 3:5). Freely and completely, Jesus saves us from an old broken life of sin and transforms us by His grace so that we can be a new creation. Old things having passed away, and all things having become new (2 Cor. 5:17).

For those who have chosen Jesus as their

Savior and Lord, the judgment will reveal that all sins have been forgiven, and that the righteousness of Jesus stands in the place of an old life of transgression. The everlasting gospel really is good news! Shouldn't everybody know about it?

SEVEN

Unforgettable Words

At a time of crisis, well-chosen words can have an enormous impact. The civil rights movement of the 1960s grew out of the bitter racism that continued to plague this nation long after the Emancipation Proclamation had been signed. As he addressed a crowd of more than 200,000 civil rights supporters, Dr. Martin Luther King, Jr. galvanized a movement with words that continue to inspire people around the world. His "I Have a Dream" speech—delivered from the steps of the Lincoln Memorial in Washington, D.C.—is widely regarded as one of the greatest speeches ever made, and it announced to the world that there was no turning back for the civil rights movement.

The Gettysburg Address—given by President Abraham Lincoln in 1863 at a time of crisis for the United States, as the Civil War continued to claim thousands of lives—contained only 272 words and took President Lincoln just over two minutes to deliver. It too is another oratorical masterpiece that continues to inspire and motivate.

A time of crisis calls for words that arrest the attention and that focus minds on which matters most. In the book of Revelation, a time of crisis causes God to respond with words that are unmistakably calculated to cause the inhabitants of planet Earth to consider subjects of eternal importance.

In addition to announcing earth's final judgment, the first angel's message in Revelation 14 goes on to call end-time believers to "worship Him who made heaven and earth, the sea and springs of water" (Rev. 14:7).

Here's a classic example of John borrowing language from the Old Testament to make a very New Testament point. The fourth commandment says, "For in six days the Lord made the heavens and the earth, the sea, and all that in them is" (Ex. 20:11). This is a clear reference to what Christ did back "in the beginning," when He called the world into existence as its Creator (Jn. 1:3; Col. 1:16). In telling us to "worship Him who made heaven and earth," John is calling us to worship Christ Jesus *as the Creator of the universe.*

Significant? Considering the context, it's absolutely significant. The previous chapter in Revelation sees the world being drawn to worship Satan—the creature, a created one. In Revelation 14, Jesus calls the world to worship Him—the Creator. And as we've seen already and will see again, the major end-time issue revolves around the question of worship.

Revelation 14:8 introduces new imagery, which John again borrowed from the Old Testament. John writes of a second angel, when he says, "And another angel followed, saying, Babylon is fallen, is fallen, that great city, because she has made all nations drink of the wine of the wrath of her fornication."

To understand the meaning of the term *Babylon*, we go back to the Old Testament—back to the time of Nimrod and the building of the Tower of Babel (or, Babylon). Babylon means "confusion," as the inhabitants of the Plain of Shinar were plunged into confusion when God confounded the language of the builders of the famed tower. Rather than following God's directions and dispersing to populate the earth, the people at Babel said, "Let us build ourselves a city, and a tower whose top is in the heavens; let us make a name for ourselves" (Gen. 11:4). This sounds much like Satan in Isaiah 14, who declared that he wanted to sit in God's place and assume God's authority.

Babylon possesses the capacity to confuse the nations of the earth, much as a person would be confused as a result of drinking wine. Imbibing the wine of Babylon results in massive spiritual confusion shortly before the return of Jesus to the world.

The ancient city of Babylon was the capital of the kingdom of Babylonia. A wealthy and powerful city, it was the seat of the greatest kingdom in the world and the home of the Hanging Gardens of Babylon, one of the seven wonders of the ancient world. Babylon was a very religious city, entirely pagan in its orientation, and it relentlessly persecuted the people of God.

When the description of Babylon given in Revelation 17 is examined, her identity becomes more obvious. She is described as a harlot, spiritually impure, and sitting upon many waters, or having authority over many people (Rev. 17:1, 15). She is pictured as sitting upon the beast with seven heads and ten horns (Rev. 17:3), an image also presented in Revelation 13:1. We discovered earlier that this beast—or, this nation—is the government of the Vatican City. Babylon is therefore clearly associated with the Vatican.

In Revelation 17:3, 4, Babylon is depicted as being clothed in purple and red, as being very wealthy, and as having daughters, while verse 6 describes her as being a persecutor of God's people.

But perhaps the most helpful clue as to Babylon's identity is that she is described as a "woman" (Rev. 17:3) and as a "harlot." In Bible prophecy, a woman is used as a symbol to represent a church (Jer. 6:2; 2 Cor. 11:2). The woman depicted in Revelation 17 is an impure woman, which represents an impure church.

So we see from the Bible that Babylon is a church system that has daughter churches, her colors are purple and red, she is wealthy, and she has persecuted God's people. In addition, she has a very close relationship with the state.

This is another biblical depiction of the first beast of Revelation 13–the papacy of the Roman Catholic Church. And in Revelation chapter 14, in the final gospel message to be presented to planet Earth, God declares that this system has "fallen." Perhaps a look at the third angel's message can help us understand why God makes such a pronouncement.

The third angel's message is also proclaimed in a "loud voice," indicating that it is of such importance that it must be announced to the whole of humankind. "If anyone worships the beast and his image, and receives his mark in his forehead or in his hand, he himself shall also drink of the wine of the wrath of God, which is poured out full strength into the cup of His indignation" (Rev. 14:9, 10).

Not a pretty picture. The Vatican evidently has a mark that is so grievous in the sight of God that it leads God to pour out His wrath "full strength." What could induce God to act in such a way?

Remember that the key issue in the time of the end is that of worship. Satan campaigned for worship and rulership in heaven, and when he was ultimately unsuccessful, he came to earth bent on receiving the worship he was not able to receive in heaven. In attempting to subvert the faith of God's people in the world's last days, Satan has built his appeal around worship.

You'll recall that in Revelation 13, Satan receives the worship of virtually the entire world. "And all who dwell upon the earth will worship him," *except* for those whose names are written in the book of life (Rev. 13:8). Who is that group worshipping?

Back to the first angel's message: "And worship Him who made heaven and earth, the sea and the springs of water" (Rev. 14:7). God calls us to worship Jesus, the Creator. But how, exactly, are we to do that?

As we noted earlier, Revelation 14:7 contains a reference from the fourth commandment, which instructs God's people to "remember the Sabbath day, to keep it holy" (Ex. 20:8). In quoting from the fourth commandment, John is clearly urging us back to keeping the seventh-day Sabbath, the same day of worship that Jesus observed.

Given to the human family at creation in the Garden of Eden, the Sabbath was a special gift of time to the human family. God says, "Come and worship me and spend special time with me." And He makes a special appointment with us, urging us to worship Him on the Sabbath day. Of course, that's not to say that God doesn't want our worship at other times, but the Sabbath is the time God set aside for people everywhere to make Himself the special center of their day.

The Sabbath wasn't an ordinance given only to the ancient Jews. In fact, Jesus Himself said, "the Sabbath was made for man" (Mk. 2:27), not simply one segment of mankind. Nor was the Sabbath set aside when Jesus died on the cross. Calvary did not make loving obedience to God obsolete. Jesus was clear when He told us that love for Him will result in a life of obedience (Jn. 14:15).

So when God asks us to "worship Him who made heaven and earth, the sea and the springs of water," He is asking us to keep the Bible Sabbath day—the seventh day—holy.

A friend of mine recently attended a lecture by a noted Catholic author. The only Protestant

in attendance, he was confronted by a gentle-
men who said to him, "If you're a Protestant, you
should be going to church on Saturday! The Bible
teaches that Saturday is the Sabbath. It was the
Catholic Church that changed the day of worship
to Sunday. If you're going to be a Protestant, you
should keep the Bible day of worship. Sunday is
our day!"

What I find to be so fascinating about this is
that what our Catholic friend said openly is rarely admitted to among Protestants. The Bible Sabbath is Saturday. Remember what the commandment says: "The seventh day is the Sabbath of the
Lord your God" (Ex. 20:10). And any dictionary
and almost all calendars will tell you that the seventh day of the week is Saturday.

As the gentleman said to my friend, the Roman
Catholic Church did change the day of worship
to Sunday and proudly admits to having done so.

"Since Saturday, not Sunday, is speci-
fied in the Bible, isn't it curious that non-
Catholics who profess to take their religion
directly from the Bible and not from the
Church, observe Sunday instead of Saturday?... They have continued the custom
even though it rests upon the authority of
the Catholic Church and not upon an ex-
plicit text from the Bible." John A. O'Brien,
The Faith of Millions, pp. 400, 401.

"Catholics learn what to believe and do
from the divine, infallible authority established by Jesus Christ, the Catholic Church,
which in apostolic times made Sunday the

day of rest to honor our Lord's resurrection on that day, and to mark off clearly the Jew from the Christian... Is it not strange that those who make the Bible their only teacher should inconsistently follow in this matter the tradition of the church?" Bertrand L. Conway, *The Question Box* (New York, NY: Missionary Society of St. Paul the Apostle, 1902).

While there is variance among scholars as to the exact time Sunday worship became established, it is clear that Sunday worship did not begin during the time of Jesus and was not generally practiced in the century or so after His death. Most important, Sunday worship did not originate with a command from God. Nowhere in the Bible does God ask anyone to keep Sunday holy. Not a single verse in the more than 31,000 verses in the Bible even comes close to being a request from God that people observe Sunday as a holy day.

But by the fourth century, Sunday worship had been established throughout much, but not all, of Christianity. The change occurred gradually. A desire arose among some Christians to appear less "Jewish" (as Jews observed the seventh-day Sabbath) and therefore avoid the persecution many Jews were experiencing. And an influx of pagans into the Christian church brought with it the practice of worshipping on the "day of the sun." When the Roman emperor Constantine was looking to consolidate his empire, he believed it would be advantageous to have a Christian empire and opted to select Sunday as the universal day for corporate worship.

Then, when the church of Rome assumed a place of ecclesiastical and then civil dominance in the world, Rome made a civil law—Sunday observance—a part of church law. Sunday worship then became a practice of the established church, endorsed by the force of the state.

Almost 1,700 years later, Sunday worship is an accepted part of society. While many millions of Christians and Jews worship on the Bible Sabbath, the vast majority of people accept Sunday as the established day of worship.

And how did we get to this point? Through the influence of the Roman Catholic Church, which—in the words of the gentleman who spoke with my good friend—changed the day of worship from Saturday to Sunday.

A good question to ask is: Who gave Rome the right to change the commandments of God? The answer is: Nobody at all. Rome assumed the authority, believing that as God's true church, it had the divinely given right to change even one of the Ten Commandments.

In fact, Rome has changed *three* of the Ten Commandments. In addition to transferring the Sabbath from the seventh day of the week, Saturday, to the first day of the week, it removed the third commandment (the prohibition against idol worship) from its catechisms and then divided the tenth commandment (regarding covetousness) into two commandments to make up for the commandment it eliminated. As Daniel 7:25 says, "He will think to change times and laws."

The idea that any church would assume the

right to alter the commandments of God is a cause for much concern. But in the eyes of the Roman church, nothing at all is wrong with what she has done, because she believes she has the authority to have done so. In fact, Rome claims that the fact she changed the Sabbath is proof of her divine mandate.

"The church is above the Bible, and this transference of Sabbath observance from Saturday to Sunday is proof positive of that fact." *The Catholic Record,* London, Ontario, September 1, 1923.

The mark of the beast isn't a barcode or a laser tattoo or a credit card or a cashless society. The mark of the beast concerns worship and is the mark or sign of the authority of the beast—the Vatican City. The mark of the beast is Sunday worship, when it is enforced by law, as stated in Revelation 13:16: "And he causeth all, both small and great, rich and poor, free and bond, to receive a mark in their right hand, or in their foreheads."

The Bible says people will be "caused," or forced, to receive the mark of the beast.

In answer to a pressing societal need—whether man-made or environmental—the mark of the beast will be offered to the world as a solution for society's ills. In a time of crisis, this act of "honoring" God will be urged upon humanity as a means of restoring to the world the blessing of God.

This will be a time of decision for everyone living on earth at that time. People will be confronted with a stark choice: the commandments of God, or the commandments of men. Obeying the beast, or obeying God. And in obeying the beast—which the vast majority of people will do—people receive into their lives the mark of the beast's authority.

Long ago in heaven, Satan rebelled against God and led one-third of heaven's angels in a revolt against the government of love. Ever since the fall of Adam and Eve, Satan has been steadily building his appeal to the human family. In Noah's day the earth was so corrupted by sin that God almost completely destroyed it.

Several times throughout history, Satan has nearly obliterated the knowledge of the true God from the earth, but in every age has been found a people who remained steadfastly faithful to God.

Yet by the Middle Ages, Christianity had descended largely into a series of forms and traditions, and true religion had all but disappeared. The medieval church had replaced faith with works, baptism by immersion with infant baptism, communion with transubstantiation, confession to God with confession to a priest, the high priestly ministry of Jesus with an earthly priesthood, and the seventh-day Sabbath with Sunday.

Though it is difficult for most people living in the twenty-first century to imagine, religious freedom didn't exist throughout much of the Middle Ages, and the power of the state was often employed to enforce the decrees of the church. The book of Revelation makes clear that history is going to repeat.

In these last days, Satan has succeeded in balancing the world precariously on the brink of ruin. Out of the uncertainty and unrest of this world, a movement will emerge that will see a leader rise to provide leadership to a world that is virtually bankrupt—financially and morally. The terrorist attacks of September 11, 2001, demonstrated that one unexpected event can set the planet heading in a radically altered direction. Society is being set up for a time of crisis, and who better to unite the world and provide leadership than this world's current undisputed moral authority?

The Bible says that Rome will assume the leadership role in a time of global crisis and will offer to the world what will be seen as a solution to a hectic life, a consumerist society, and a spiritually bereft existence. A day of rest—an idea so good that God thought of it first—will be offered to a world in need of that very thing. But Rome will offer the world the day of rest of her devising, and not God's. Instead of honoring God, the day of rest—the mark of the beast's authority—will dishonor God and lead people into disobedience and conflict with the will and word of the Almighty.

And in this final crisis, Jesus stands as the true solution to the world's needs. As society becomes increasingly wayward and drifts farther and still farther from God's ideals, the solution to its woes is a total commitment to the principles of heaven. The mark of the beast will be offered as the solution to the world's ills, while the three angels of Revelation 14 call the world to the worship of the Creator, with the Sabbath—given at Creation—

standing as a memorial of God's power to create and recreate.

While it is important to know the finer points of the prophecy of Revelation chapter 14, at its heart the message of the chapter is simple. A spiritual crisis is coming to the world. While the world is seeking a solution to this crisis, the real solution is Jesus, "the Way, the Truth and the Life" (Jn. 14:6). Only a complete surrender to Jesus will enable a person to stand in this planet's final, tumultuous time. Only adherence to God's Word—and not to man's interpretation of God's Word—will enable us to have the faith necessary to stand when the world is coming apart. Simple trust in Jesus is all that is necessary to see a person stand one soon day on heaven's streets of gold.

You can have that faith in Jesus today.

EIGHT

Armageddon

T he most popular movie of 1998 was *Arma-geddon,* the story of the efforts of a NASA team trying to stop a huge asteroid collid-ing with our planet. Starring Bruce Willis, "Ar-mageddon" earned more money at the box office that year than any other movie, including the Steven Spielberg epic, *Saving Private Ryan.* The movie's plot suggested that if the asteroid were to strike the earth, there would be massive devasta-tion—Armageddon.

The word *Armageddon* is commonly used to refer to destruction on a massive scale. It is re-ported that during his presidency, Ronald Reagan believed Armageddon was near for the United States. A potential nuclear war is frequently re-ferred to as "Armageddon," while in 2011, a new word entered the lexicon of Californians, when a large road construction project was expected to result in "Carmageddon."

In the Bible, the word *Armageddon* appears

in the context of the seven last plagues that fall shortly before Jesus' Second Coming. The plagues are judgments that fall upon those "which had the mark of the beast" (Rev. 16:2)—people who, in a time of spiritual crisis, made the decision to follow the commandments of man rather than those of God.

Revelation 16 doesn't make for easy reading. Seven fearsome plagues are visited upon the rejecters of God's mercy and grace. And this might make a person wonder why God would do something so severe.

When God sends the plagues, is He simply punishing people for not obeying Him? Is God acting the part of an angered parent who "just can't take it anymore"?

If God has simply lost His patience with the world, we could certainly question His fairness. In fact, a characteristic of God's saved people in the last days is that they have "patience" (Rev. 14:12), and surely God can be expected to play by His own rules.

So why the plagues? Why would God send judgments of sores, bloody water and a scorching sun, among other things? Keep in mind that this will not be the first time God has sent plagues upon the earth. Ten plagues fell in Egypt, as Moses was preparing to lead God's people out of captivity and on toward the Promised Land.

At that time, God's people were being horribly oppressed by a heathen ruler, the Egyptian Pharaoh, and were being held against their will in the land of their enemies. Before liberating His people, God would give Pharaoh every possible chance to repent of his wickedness and yield to the true God. In this great controversy between Christ and Satan, God wants not only to be just ,but also to be seen to be just. Rather than simply leading His people out of Egypt, God gave Pharaoh every inducement to choose to serve Him.

Each of the ten plagues that fell in Egypt were a revelation to Pharaoh of the sovereignty of God. In fact, as you read the story in the book of Exodus, you discover that Pharaoh was convinced he was in opposition to the God of the universe. "I have sinned against the Lord your God, and against you," Pharaoh said. "Entreat the Lord your God that he may take away from me this death only" (Ex. 10:16, 17).

Each plague impressed upon the mind of Pharaoh that he was standing in opposition to Someone far greater than he, and that God was inviting him to repent and be saved. Pharaoh squandered that opportunity, and unlike the heathen king Nebuchadnezzar—who responded to revelations of God's goodness (Dan. 4:37)—Pharaoh died a lost man.

So in sending the seven last plagues, is God giving those with the mark of the beast the opportunity to repent? No, He is not. The seven last plagues are visited upon those who have received the mark of the beast, having utterly and irrevocably rejected God's invitation to come under the covering of His grace. In sending the plagues, God is revealing to the world what the character of the lost is really like. And in sending the plagues, God also reveals the makeup of the character of the saved.

This will be a time of intense difficulty and hardship. What is a person to do when afflicted with terrible sores? What is a person to drink, when drinking water turns to blood? What happens to a global economy, when the seas become as the blood of a dead man and ocean travel becomes impossible?

Without question, the lost will experience incredible difficulty and, like Pharaoh, will be confronted with the question of their relationship to the God of heaven. Yet, instead of coming to their senses and apologizing to God and appealing for forgiveness, the lost blaspheme and insult God and will "not repent to give Him glory" (Rev. 16:9, 11). Even when confronted with their utterly lost condition, the lost refuse to repent. They are beyond hope and are not safe to save into the kingdom of heaven.

And what of the righteous? The righteous at this time must pass through a time of great trial. The entire population of the world is now divided into two groups—those who have received the mark of the beast and are receiving the plagues, and those who are sealed with the seal of God and are shielded from receiving the plagues.

The saved must therefore be the objects of the wrath and hatred of the lost. Having chosen to stand in opposition to the vast majority of people alive, this small group is now protected at a time when the majority is afflicted.

The seven last plagues demonstrate that the saved are prepared to lean entirely upon Jesus at a time of unimaginable stress and difficulty. While already sealed with the seal of God, the attitude of the saved under such intense pressure reveals to the universe that, unlike the lost, they are ready for translation.

Far from being a literal battle in an Israeli valley, Armageddon represents the final global confrontation between the forces of evil and the company of the redeemed. Satan has long wanted to rid the world of any evidence that God is love, and here, on the edge of eternity, one final group of people continues to cling by faith to the God of heaven. But before Satan can marshal the wicked to finally exterminate the righteous, the seventh plague falls, causing massive destruction to the earth and heralding the greatest event since the creation of the world—the Second Coming of Jesus.

It is said that the first book of the Bible to be written was the book of Job, written by Moses some time before he wrote the book of Genesis. Yet, even Job looked longingly to the Second Coming of Jesus—the event described by Titus as "that blessed hope" (Ti. 2:13). Job said, "I know that my Redeemer liveth, and that he shall stand at the latter day upon the earth. And though after my skin worms destroy this body, yet in my flesh shall I see God. Whom I shall see for myself, and mine eyes shall behold" (Job 19:25-27).

Jesus said, in John 14:3, "I will come again and receive you unto myself." Believers have clung for millennia to the hope that Jesus will one day return and on that day put an end to the sin and sadness that have afflicted this world for thousands of years.

After the depiction of the falling of the plagues in Revelation 16 and the rebellion of Babylon in Revelation 17 and 18, we are presented with John's vision of the Second Coming of Jesus, the climax of the book of Revelation.

John writes, "And I saw heaven opened, and behold a white horse, and He that sat upon him was called Faithful and True, and in righteousness He doth judge and make war. His eyes were as a flame of fire, and on His head were many crowns; and He had a name written, that no man knew, but He Himself. And He was clothed with a vesture dipped in blood: and His name is called The Word of God" (Rev. 19:11-13).

This awe-inspiring picture of Jesus lets us know that one day soon, Jesus will put an end to the ages-long battle between good and evil, between Christ and Satan.

"And the armies which were in heaven followed Him upon white horses, clothed in fine linen, white and clean. And out of His mouth goeth a sharp sword, that with it He should smite the nations: and He shall rule them with a rod of iron: and He treadeth the winepress of the fierceness and wrath of Almighty God. And He hath on His vesture and on His thigh a name written, King of Kings, and Lord of Lords" (Rev. 19:14-16).

The moment God's waiting saints have long been anticipating is finally here. The heavens depart as a scroll (Rev. 6:14), and Jesus is seen riding down the great corridors of space, accompanied by the angels of heaven.

The redeemed cry out with hearts full of joy, "Lo, this is our God. We have waited for Him and He will save us. This is the Lord; we have waited for Him, we will be glad and rejoice in His salvation" (Isa. 25:9). Gravity will no longer be permitted to keep the feet of God's people connected with the earth. As Paul wrote, "The Lord Himself shall descend from heaven with a shout, with the voice of the archangel, and with the trump of God: and the dead in Christ shall rise first" (1 Thess. 4:16).

What a reunion day this will be! The saved of all ages who died prior to this time will be raised from the dead, and with the living saints will be changed "in a moment, in the twinkling of an eye, at the last trump: for the trumpet shall sound, and the dead shall be raised incorruptible, and we shall be changed" (1 Cor. 15:52).

God has long assured us that we will see our loved ones again. Husbands will be reunited with wives, children with parents, and brothers with sisters. Jesus has returned! The dead in Christ are risen, and along with the living redeemed, they begin their journey to heaven. "And if I go and prepare a place for you, I will come again to receive you unto myself; that where I am, there you may be also" (Jn. 14:3).

For the lost, the Second Coming has an altogether different effect. In Revelation 6, the lost are depicted as crying out to the mountains and rocks to fall on them and "hide us from the face of Him that sitteth on the throne, and from the wrath of the Lamb" (Rev. 6:16).

Isn't it curious that a person would want to hide from a lamb? I've had pet lambs. They're about as docile an animal as you would ever want to know. Yet people are fleeing from a lamb—or, a Lamb.

When Jesus is revealed at the Second Coming, His glory is welcomed by those who have been transformed by the Holy Spirit and have developed a character like the character of Christ. But for those whose hearts are not connected with Jesus, this display of His majesty will be more than they can bear. They are destroyed by the brightness of His glory.

The return of Jesus marks the beginning of the millennium—the 1,000-year period discussed in Revelation 20. For 1,000 years, God's people enjoy the glory of heaven, finally free to live in a land without sin. At the end of the millennium, the redeemed return to the earth, which will be recreated following the final, irrevocable destruction of the wicked.

"For behold," God says, "I create new heavens and a new earth: and the former shall not be remembered, nor come into mind" (Isa. 65:17). "And God shall wipe away all tears from their eyes; and there shall be no more death, neither sorrow, nor crying, neither shall there be any more pain: for the former things are passed away" (Rev. 21:4).

Finally, the earth is returned to the condition God always intended for it to enjoy. And as much as the redeemed will enjoy this unfathomable blessing, there is One who will be happiest of all. For thousands of years, sin has marred God's universe. It has cost Him one-third of the angels He created, and it has cost Him the life of His own Son, Jesus.

But now sin is gone, and as the prophet Nahum wrote, "Affliction will not rise up the second time" (Nah. 1:9). Finally, God is able to dwell with His people.

At Creation, the sin suggested to the world by the serpent caused separation to come between God and humanity (Isa. 59:2). During the wilderness wandering, God dwelt among His people in the sanctuary (Ex. 25:8), but apostasy and rebellion caused God to vacate the structures made for Him by His people. And the Bible records that when Jesus came to the world to tabernacle among the fallen human family (Jn. 1:14, *Young's Literal Translation*), "He came unto His own, and His own received Him not" (Jn. 1:11).

But now God's desire to dwell in the midst of His people becomes a reality. His followers have leaned on Jesus, in spite of pressing difficulties, and have remained faithful in the midst of incredible pressure to compromise

John writes, in Revelation 21:3, "Behold, the tabernacle of God is with men, and He will dwell with them, and they shall be His people, and God Himself shall be with them, and be their God."

The book of Revelation, as no other book, takes us on a journey through history and into the future, revealing to us that faith in Christ will see us through any hardship or trial that may come to us. One day, Jesus is going to return. One day, sin will be no more. One day, we'll live in a land where the flowers never fade, enjoying communion with the God of the universe.

Beyond the beasts, beyond the symbols and the signs, we see a loving Savior, graciously inviting us to lean on Him every day of our lives, to trust Him for forgiveness, and to follow Him even when induced to do otherwise.

Jesus is soon to return to this earth. Eternity stretches before us. Understanding the big picture—the panorama of Bible prophecy—believers in Jesus can look to the future with confidence and live today with the assurance that God is love.

We can live with the expectation that soon, we will enjoy the eternal blessing of God. This isn't merely a pipe dream or a wish. This is the promise God makes to us and gives us through the Star of the book of Revelation—today.

HAVE QUESTIONS?

FIND ANSWERS

Can God be trusted? Is there hope for our planet? What must we do to have eternal life? Why does God allow suffering? Can we understand Bible prophecy? Find answers to these and other questions—straight from the Bible!

The **It Is Written Bible Study Guides** feature 25 lessons that use a simple fill-in-the-blank format, with an answer key included. The complete set is available for only $9.99 (plus shipping).

To order, please call toll-free 1-888-664-5573. Or order online from our website at **www.itiswritten.com/biblestudy**.

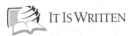 IT IS WRITTEN

www.itiswritten.com

 facebook.com/itiswritten

 twitter.com/itiswritten

About It Is Written

It Is Written is an international television ministry dedicated to sharing insights from God's Word with people around the world. Founded in 1956 by George Vandeman, the theme of this Christian ministry can be found in Matthew 4:4: "It is written, 'Man shall not live by bread alone, but by every word that proceeds from the mouth of God.'"

The warm conversational style of speaker/director John Bradshaw addresses contemporary issues in a refreshing new way. Each week, Pastor Bradshaw takes timeless biblical truths and applies them to everyday life.

Programs regularly deal with issues such as loneliness, fear, low self-esteem, health, family values and spiritual principles. People of all faiths and creeds—even those with no faith at all—have been inspired and encouraged through It Is Written's straightforward, Christ-centered presentations.

Prayer and a commitment to impacting the world for God have sent It Is Written's television signal beaming around the globe. It Is Written airs on TBN, 3ABN, the Hope Channel and hundreds of other stations in 130 countries around the world.

To learn more, please visit It Is Written online, where you can watch the weekly program, find your local station, use our free, interactive Bible studies, purchase Christian resources and find upcoming It Is Written events in your area. Simply visit www.itiswritten.com.

IT IS WRITTEN

PO Box 6, Chattanooga, TN 37401 • (423) 362-5800
www.itiswritten.com